Often when we discuss the effects of taxes, we focus on the effects on the mean of firm value and de-emphasize the effects on the variance of the distribution. The existing literature on dividend taxation has analyzed the effect on firm stock price (Auerbach and Hassett (2005) and Amromin, Harrison and Sharpe (2008)). However, there are two important moments for the stock: the level of the stock price and the volatility of the stock. In a world where executives are more risk averse than most shareholders (since they are unable to diversify away firm-specific risk), we want to focus on both the mean and the variance effects due to agency costs. If a dividend tax change sufficiently increases volatility, the executive may take actions to decrease the volatility of the stock at the expense of the share price. Therefore, the stock price might not increase as much as it would have in a world with risk-neutral executives (or equally risk averse executives and shareholders). It is therefore important to consider the effects on the volatility of the stock.

In many models of stock valuation, general shareholders are able to diversify the idiosyncratic risk of a stock and are thus only affected by systematic risk. However, one important class of shareholders is often unable to diversify the idiosyncratic risk: executives.[1] A board of directors will set optimal incentives for their executives that include undiversifiable risk so that executives have an incentive to increase the firm's value. However, when executives are unable to diversify the idiosyncratic risk, they will be negatively affected by an increase in volatility due to a change in the tax environment. In a world where taxes change the second moment, without any changes in company policy, the welfare of the shareholders would be unaffected. Because the welfare of the managers would be affected by the second moment

---

[1]There is a large theoretical literature starting with Jensen and Meckling (1976) that demonstrates the trade-off between incentives and risk. In a traditional agency model, the executive takes firm risk as given and incentives are negatively correlated with firm risk, which Jin (2002), Aggarwal and Samwick (1999), Core and Guay (1999), and Core and Guay (2002b) empirically evaluate.

effects, the tax change could affect the principal–agent costs associated with the hiring of manager.[2]

One particular channel through which an executive may affect volatility is through investment.[3] For example, the principal–agent costs could be particularly large if an increase in investment leads to an increase in variance in the distribution of firm output. In this case, the risk-averse executive would benefit from investing but would have the cost of an increase in the variance.[4] The shareholders would only have the benefit from the investment. Therefore, they would want the executive to increase the investment, but the executive would increase the investment by less than the shareholder's optimal amount due to the additional variance costs. This difference would exacerbate the original agency costs.

Previous theoretical research has shown that taxes may affect the volatility of a stock in both the traditional manner, such as through firm capital structure, and through agency-based mechanisms. In a traditional model such as in Modigliani and Miller (1958), taxes may also change the financial structure of a firm. A decrease in the dividend tax may make debt less desirable and equity more desirable.[5] If firms move toward more equity, the volatility of their equity might decrease.

Agency models predict that dividends are used to decrease agency costs at the firm.[6] If

---

[2]Examples of costs associated with volatility include hedging (Knopf, Nam and Thorton (2002)) and changes in leverage (Coles, Daniel and Naveen (2006) and Chava and Purnanandam (2010)).

[3]See Lambert (1986), Hirshleifer and Suh (1992), Knopf et al. (2002), and Coles et al. (2006) for agency effects on investment.

[4]While the executive's options portfolio would increase in value with increased stock variance, this is a second-order effect.

[5]See Graham (2003); Auerbach (2002); Graham (1996); and MacKie-Mason (1990) for theoretical and empirical implications.

[6]If the firm pays dividends, then it will have less cash on hand to use for overinvestment by the executive. Christie and Nanda (1994) find lower dividend growth in firms with higher agency costs as the firms had high dividends originally to mitigate some of the high agency costs. La Porta, de Silanes, Schleifer and Vishny (2000) and Fenn and Liang (2001) also find evidence in support of the agency theory.

dividends are used to decrease agency costs by decreasing overinvestment at a firm, a decrease in the dividend tax may decrease agency costs and lead to a decrease in overinvestment. In addition, if dividends are used as a signal, a decrease in taxes on dividends decreases the price of the signal (Bernheim and Wantz (1995) and Bernheim and Redding (2001)).

Previous theoretical and empirical papers have considered whether a dividend tax change affects initiation and size of dividends. Empirically, Blouin, Raedy and Shackelford (2007) and Brown, Liang and Weisbenner (2007) found that firms changed their payout policy from share repurchases to paying dividends after a dividend tax change. Agency models also suggest that in addition to the overall effect of tax changes, there should be a differential effect for firms with the largest incentives relative to firms with fewer incentives.[7] Chetty and Saez (2005); Nam, Wang and Zhang (2004); and Brown et al. (2007) provide empirical evidence of the agency mechanism.

This paper builds on the existing literature by identifying the effects of a tax change on stock volatility and compensation. Specifically, I find that the variance decreased more for firms with highly incentivized executives relative to firms with less highly incentivized executives. A measure of variance is the daily volatility of the stock. However, this volatility comprises two pieces. The first is the firm-specific idiosyncratic volatility. The second is the systematic volatility, associated with overall market movements. I separate these two pieces by looking at the error from a daily Fama-French Three-Factor Model regression. I then look at the quarterly volatility of this error to examine whether the volatility increased after the 2003 tax cut. Therefore, I take a difference-in-differences approach where I compare the volatility of firms who have executives with incentives in the lowest–quintile to firms who have

---

[7]See Chetty and Saez (2010) and Gordon and Dietz (2006) for examples related to a dividend tax change.

executives with incentives in the highest–quintile. I find that firms with executives in the highest–quintile of incentives had the largest decrease in both systematic and idiosyncratic volatility after the 2003 tax change. The results are robust to specifying the volatility in returns or in price. Dividend taxes appear to affect firm volatility. Because they may exacerbate agency costs, we should consider the effects on the firm's stock price volatility when changing tax policies.

# 1 Background on Relevant Tax Changes and Hypothesis Development

The Jobs and Growth Tax Relief Reconciliation Act of 2003 changed many aspects of the U.S. tax code. President Bush proposed the legislation on January 7, 2003, and Congress passed the bill by the end of May. It was made retroactive to January 1, 2003. In particular, it temporarily decreased both the long-term capital gains tax rate and the dividend tax rate. The capital gains tax rate was reduced from a maximum rate of 20% to 15%. The larger change was in the dividend tax: The qualified dividend tax rate fell from a maximum rate of 35% to a maximum rate of 15%.[8] This law disproportionately decreased the dividend tax rate for individuals with high incomes, as the dividend tax rate decreased from the executive's personal income rate (35%) to a maximum of 15%. It is therefore a change which can be used to study the effects of dividend taxation on stock volatility, through the effect on executive behavior.

---

[8]See Auten, Carroll and Gee (2008) for a detailed description of all the tax changes associated with the 2003 law.

The rhetoric before the dividend tax cut followed two different molds. The first said that the dividend tax cut would increase investment for all firms as the cost of capital decreases. Investors will therefore invest more in firms which will increase the value of all firms. However, if investment leads to higher volatility in firm earnings, then it should also increase the volatility of the stocks.

The second mold was that the dividend tax would decrease overinvestment in non-value enhancing projects by executives and increase corporate governance by increasing the incentive to disburse earnings through dividends. This would decrease volatility.

Both molds would affect both the price and the volatility of the stock. If executives are more risk averse than shareholders and the executives receive some compensation in the form of stock and options, then executives are similarly aligned with shareholders on price but may be misaligned on volatility. Options could offset some of this misalignment as the value of each option increases with the volatility of the stock. If the dividend tax change led to an increase in the volatility for all firms, the changes should be the smallest for the firms where an executive had a large portion of his compensation in the form of stock. On the other hand, for firms where an executive has a significant portion of his compensation in options, the change in volatility should be largest.

The dividend tax change differentially affects volatility by level of executive incentive. An executive who has a significant amount of their pay tied to the price of a stock faces a significant amount of risk if the value of that stock decreases. If the executive is risk averse and their compensation contract includes a significant amount of stock or options, the executive will take both the stock price and the stock's volatility into his optimization strategy for the firm. The executive may then choose between giving out a larger dividend

5

or investing in the firm (or holding cash at the firm), which will affect the volatility of the firm's stock's price.

**Hypothesis 1.** *The increase (decrease) in the volatility of a stock after an increase (decrease) in the dividend tax rate is larger in magnitude for firms with larger incentives.*

On the one hand, if the executive has a large holding of shares, he faces a larger cost of dispersing dividends if the dividend tax increases. Therefore, he may decrease dividends more than an executive with fewer shares would, which will affect both the stock price and the firm's volatility. There will be a differential effect of the stock volatility for firms with executives with large incentives.

On the other hand, if an executive has a large number of options (given his price sensitivity), he has an incentive to increase both the share price and the volatility of the stock.

**Hypothesis 2.** *The decrease (increase) in the volatility of a stock after an increase (decrease) in the dividend tax rate is larger in magnitude for firms with a larger number of options.*

If the executive has a large holding of options, then he has an incentive to increase the volatility of the stock. Therefore, he may increase dividends more than an executive with fewer options would, which will affect both the stock price and the firm's volatility. There will be a differential effect of the stock volatility for firms with executives with a large number of options.

# 2  Data

## 2.1  Data Sources

The primary data source for this paper is from the Center for Research in Security Prices (CRSP). This data source includes daily prices for stocks. It also includes the timing of the payment of dividends and the type of dividend paid by each firm for each day. I merge this data with data from Compustat on firm finances. The last data source is the ExecuComp Database, which includes information on compensation for the five highest–paid executives of each firm in the S&P 1500. This limits my data to firms in the S&P 1500. There is partial data for 1992, but the full sample begins in 1993, so I consider all firms in the S&P 1500 from 1993 to 2013. In order to avoid changes in sample composition over time, firms must be in the ExecuComp database in 2000, and must include data on several variables including total assets and net income. These requirements limit the sample to 1,465 firms.[9] Compustat includes quarterly financial data, so there are a total of 88,457 firm-quarter observations in the sample.

The S&P 1500 contains 500 large market capitalization firms, 400 middle market capitalization firms, and 600 small market capitalization firms. Market capitalization is defined as the number of common shares outstanding at the end of the quarter times the closing price at the end of the quarter. Table 1 includes summary statistics for the firms in the sample. Price is the price variable from CRSP at the close of the market on the last day of the quarter. As expected, there is a large dispersion in prices, with prices ranging from 5 cents

---

[9]The number of firms in CRSP may differ, as the matching CRSP ID changes over time for a few firms in the sample.

to over a hundred thousand dollars. However, the mean is about 82 dollars, and most firms do not have extreme prices. Also, as expected for the S&P 1500, there is a large dispersion in market capitalization. The smallest firm has a market capitalization of just above 2.5 million dollars, while the largest firm has a market capitalization of over 626 billion dollars. Profit margin is defined as yearly net income divided by yearly sales for the most recent 12 months. Most firms make a positive profit of about 7 cents per dollar of sales. The firms earn, on average, 1.08 cents per share, but this is much more dispersed than profit margin. Sales per share is defined on a yearly basis. There is a large dispersion in the overall sales per share. The market–to–book ratio averages 1.86 but ranges from 0.3 to 74.5.[10] The leverage ratio is the long–term debt divided by total assets. The average firm has a leverage ratio of 0.2, with some firms not financed at all by debt and other firms heavily financed by debt. The Earnings Quality measure is the measure used in Rajgopal and Venkatachalam (2011); they find that it can significantly affect firm stock price volatility. [11] This measure varies significantly for the firms-quarters in this sample.

## 2.2    Volatility Measures

An executive's utility includes the value of his take-home pay, which may include incentive pay. If the incentive pay varies with the stock market, then the take-home pay of the executive will vary with the stock market. Furthermore, if he is risk averse, then an increase

---

[10]As in Malmendier and Tate (2009), I define market to book value as the ratio of Market Value of Assets to Book Value of Assets. Book value of assets is total assets at the end of the quarter. Market value of assets is defined as Book Value of Assets plus market equity minus book equity. Market equity is defined as common shares outstanding at the end of the quarter times quarter closing price. Book equity is calculated as stockholders equity at the end of the quarter [or the first available of common equity outstanding plus preferred stock par value or total assets minus total liabilities ] minus preferred stock liquidating value.

[11]The authors use a measure developed by Dechow and Dichev (2002) that is based on an estimate for total accruals.

in the volatility of take-home pay would negatively impact his utility. The standard deviation

of his take-home pay can be approximated as the volatility of number of shares that he owns

through stock options and times the price. I have four possible proxies for the volatility of

take-home pay. Two measures consider the standard deviation of the stock return over a

quarter. The other two measures consider the standard deviation of the stock price over a

quarter. If the number of shares is negatively correlated with the price of the shares, then

the standard deviation of the return may be the best measure to use.[12] However, if the

number of shares is not negatively correlated with price, then the volatility of price may be

the best measure to use.[13] In the data, I find the correlation between stock price and the

level of incentives to be 0.4. It is highly significant with a t-statistic of 19.8. Therefore, the

price and the overall level of incentives seems to be positively correlated, and the volatility

of price is the best measure to use. I focus on this measure but also include the standard

deviation of the stock price return.

In addition to the price-return breakdown, I also consider the difference between the

---

[12]Consider two stocks, a high–priced stock and a low–priced stock, that increase by exactly 1% every other day and decrease to the original prices (approximately a 0.99% decrease) on the other days. After the quarter (assuming an even number of days again), the price of the stocks is equal to the price at the start of the quarter. The overall return is zero. Both the low–price stock and the high–price stock will have the same standard deviation of returns. However, the low–price stock will have a much higher standard deviation of price than the high–price stock. If the executives of both the high– and low–price stock have the same number of shares of the high and low stock, the volatility of both executive's income is higher for the executive with the high–priced share as a 1% increase is larger for a high–priced share than a low–priced share. However, if the executive of the low–priced stock has the number of shares required to make his shares value the same amount as the high–priced stock executive, then the two would have the same volatility of income

[13]Now consider two stocks that increase by exactly a dollar every other day. On the days when they do not increase by a dollar, they decrease by exactly a dollar. After a quarter (assuming an even number of days), the stocks would have the same prices as at the beginning of the quarter. If one stock has a high price and one has a low price, the volatility of the stock price will be exactly the same for the two stocks. However, the volatility of the return would be much higher for the stock with a low price compared to the stock with a high price. If the executives of both the high and low priced stock have the same number of share of the high and low priced stock, the volatility of both executive's income is the same. However, if the executive of the low priced stock has more shares, the volatility of his income is higher.

standard deviation and the excess standard deviation. The standard deviation of either the price or the return can be broken into two pieces. One piece is the systematic volatility. The other piece is the idiosyncratic volatility. The overall market may increase or decrease due to general market conditions. A firm may either move with or against the market (or not with the market at all). The executive may have little control over this piece of the volatility. However, the firm also will have an idiosyncratic error, which the executive may have more control over.[14] In addition, the type of firm (whether it is a pro-cyclical or anti-cyclical firm) may have been previously determined. Therefore, although the executive's income will increase or decrease with the overall volatility of the market, the piece of the volatility that he may have control over is the excess volatility.

I define all four measures of standard deviation: the standard deviation of the price of the stock, the standard deviation of the stock return, the standard deviation of the stock's excess return, and the excess standard deviation of the stock price. All four are measured over the course of the quarter and consider daily changes in the stock's value.[15]

Figure 1 includes the quarterly average for each of the four measures from 1993 to 2013. For the basic measure, the quarterly standard deviation of the daily price, the measure generally increases through 1998. It then falls until 2001, at which point it remains relatively constant until the financial crisis in 2008 when it spikes. It then returns to a lower level in 2010, where it plateaus through the remainder of the series. This measure does not control for any market changes, and only considers overall volatility of the price. After controlling for some market changes by looking at the standard deviation of the price error, the pattern

---

[14]Let's say he can choose either a high–risk or low–risk project. The volatility would increase or decrease but it may or may not be correlated with the overall market. The executive may also be able to increase or decrease overall risk by changing the size of the investment.

[15]See Appendix A.1 for definitions.

is the same; each of the volatilities is smaller however. The standard deviation of the return is much smaller than the standard deviation of the price. It generally rises through 2000 and then generally falls through 2003. As with the price measure, it increases dramatically in the financial crisis, before falling and stabilizing in 2010. Again, this measure does not control for any market changes. If we control for market changes by looking at the standard deviation of the return error, the volatility decreases.

## 2.3 Incentive Measures

The above volatility measures estimate the overall and idiosyncratic volatility of the stock price. As discussed above, the optimal choice of the volatility measure depends on the executive's pay package. Therefore, I need a measure of how the executive's take-home pay increases with either a dollar increase in stock price or a 1% increase in the stock price. For many firms, the executive's pay package includes a salary, stock grants, and stock options. Both the stock grants' and the stock options' value depend upon the stock price. Therefore, a one-dollar increase in the stock price will increase both the value of the stock grants and the stock options. For each share that the executive owns, a one–dollar increase in the stock price will increase the value of the executive's stock portfolio by one–dollar. The change in the value of an option for a dollar increase in the value of the underlying stock varies based on the time remaining for the option and how far the stock price is from the strike price of the option if the option is valued using the Black-Scholes formula. Therefore, it does not have a dollar-for-dollar increase in the value of the option for each dollar increase in the stock price. One needs to combine both the increase from the stock grants and the increase in the value from the option grants. To accurately estimate this value, one needs information on each of the options the executive owns. This information includes the strike price and the time remaining. The yearly proxy statement that a public firm is required to submit to the Securities and Exchange Commission unfortunately does not include this information. It does, however, include information on the value of the options that are in the money, on the value of the options that are out of the money, on the number of options that are in the money, and on the number of options that are out of the money. In addition it includes information on the stock options granted that year.

Core and Guay (2002a) developed a methodology for estimating the effect of a 1% increase in the stock price on the value of an executive's overall portfolio, called the sensitivity to price. I use this methodology to estimate the effects of a stock price change on the executive's take-home pay. If the stock price is more volatile and the executive has a large sensitivity to price, then the executive's take-home pay will be more volatile than the take-home pay of an executive with either a smaller stock price volatility or a smaller sensitivity to price.

In addition to the effect of a change in the volatility of the stock on the volatility of the take-home pay, the volatility of the stock enters directly into the valuation of a stock option through the Black-Scholes formula. If a stock has a high volatility, it is more likely to have a day where it is valued far above the strike price. Therefore, the value of an option increases with the volatility of the stock. Core and Guay (2002a) also develop a methodology for estimating the effect of a 0.01 increase in the stock-return volatility on the valuation of all options in the executive's portfolio called the sensitivity to volatility. If an executive owns a large number of options relative to the number of shares of stock, an increase in the volatility of the stock will increase the value of the executive's portfolio more than for an executive who has fewer options in his incentive portfolio.

For much of the empirical section, the sensitivities are broken into quintiles for the year 2000 for the executive with the highest sensitivity at the firm. One question is, how does the sensitivity increase by quintile? In Table 2, the sensitivity to price increases from zero (the executive owns no stock or options) to $585,400 on average. The first quintile has executives who do not have much sensitivity to price. A 1% increase in the stock price would increase the average executive's take-home pay by 15 dollars, and the executive with the largest effect would only have take-home pay increased by 40 dollars. Compared to average executive salaries, these numbers are very small. The next quintile includes executives whose take-home pay would increase from 40 dollars to 137 dollars. Again, these are not large relative to overall compensation. The average in the third quintile is still only 244 dollars. In the fourth quintile take-home pay begins to be affected more, but the maximum is still only 1,161 dollars. The large effects are only found in the last quintile. Here, a 1% increase in price increases the take-home by almost 10,000 dollars on average. Note that this dollar amount in the top quintile is much smaller than the dollar amount for the top sensitivity to price quintile. It is also relatively small given the average take-home pay for the executives. This quintile has large incentive pay, and executives in it may act differently than executives in the other quintiles.

Table 2 also includes information on the sensitivity to volatility. Here, 507 of the firms do not include any options in their pay packages, so the executive's take-home pay is not influenced directly by volatility. Again, only a small fraction of the executives have a large increase in the value of take-home pay for a 0.01 increase in volatility. The bottom four quintiles are all less than 55 dollars. The top quintile ranges from 55 dollars to 4,536 dollars.

13

The effects here are also pretty small compared to the effects for sensitivity to price.

Given that there are two measures based on how the executives are paid, the sensitivity to price and sensitivity to volatility might be strongly correlated if options are driving the sensitivity to price. However, I find that the correlation is only 0.03. The correlation between quintiles is 0.44. Table 3 includes the number of firms in each quintile for sensitivity to price broken down by what quintile of sensitivity to volatility they are in. There is some correlation in the table. There are no firms that have executives with the highest sensitivity to volatility but the lowest sensitivity to price. Given that firms that have executives with a high sensitivity to volatility also must have a large number of options, this is understandable. On the other hand, the firms who have executives with a high sensitivity to price are relatively spread out by volatility quintile for the first four quintiles. As expected, there are more in the fifth quintile. Therefore, there is some correlation between the two but it is not a one-for-one movement.

# 3    Empirical Strategy and Results

To empirically evaluate whether a decrease in the dividend tax will cause less of an increase in the volatility of the stock for firms with executives who have larger incentives to begin with (Hypothesis 1), I use the measure of the sensitivity of executives' stock and option holdings to price defined in Section 2.3. Following the methodology from Chetty and Saez (2010), for each firm, I consider the five executives in the ExecuComp Database in 2000. I then compare the sensitivity to price for each of the five executives. I find the executive who has the largest sensitivity to price for the firm. The year 2000 was chosen because it was before President Bush was elected. President Bush was one of the major supporters of the dividend tax change and discussed it before pursuing the legislation. Therefore, the board of directors for any given firm may not have taken the tax change into account by 2000. I am interested in the volatility of take-home pay for the executives. Take-home pay for the executives depends upon both the valuation of the stock and the valuation of options. Volatility depends on the stock price, and the volatility of take-home pay depends on the volatility of price. Therefore, the overall sensitivity of take-home pay to stock price is the optimal measure here. As in Chetty and Saez (2010), I consider quintiles of sensitivity to price. I group the firms into five groups based on the maximum sensitivity to price for all five executives in the ExecuComp database in 2000. Using these quintiles interacted with time leads to a difference-in-differences approach. This avoids several typical time-series identification problems as I can add time–fixed effects. If there are time-series changes that are associated with the incentive scheme, this difference–in–differences approach will not be identified. In addition, if there are other contemporaneous effects, I will be unable to separate the two. I also provide evidence that the timing of the effects occurs at the beginning of 2003, exactly at the time of the tax change.

I test this by examining the effect of the decrease in the dividend tax rate in 2003. Using the quintiles of highest sensitivity to price for the top five executives per firm in 2000, I have a measure of the incentive schemes for the executives with the largest incentive schemes. Therefore, the firms with executives who are in Quintile 5 should experience a greater negative effect on volatility than the firms with executives in other quintiles. Quintile 4 should be more negative than Quintile 3 which should be more negative than Quintile 2, which in turn should be more negative than Quintile 1. Therefore, one can look at the changes in volatility for the firms, and one can compare across quintiles.

Section 2.2 describes four volatility measures. The standard deviation of the excess price is the optimal measure. Therefore, I focus on the standard deviation of excess price measure. The other three measures lead to similar results. Table 4 estimates the following equation:

$$log(sd(\Delta p)_{iqy}) = \gamma_i + \beta_1 log(p_{iqy}) + \beta_2 X_{iqy} + \eta_d \quad (1)$$

$$+ \sum_{n=1}^{5} (\beta_{3n} D_{qy} * QP_{in}) + \sum_{l=1}^{5} (\beta_{4l} D_{qy} * QV_{il}) + \epsilon_{iqy},$$

where $log(sd(\Delta p)_{iqy})$ is the log of the standard deviation of the stock $i$ price error for day $t$ in fiscal quarter $q$ in fiscal year $y$. $X_{iqy}$ are firm variables that previous literature has indicated affect volatility, $\gamma_i$ is a firm–fixed effect, $\eta_d$ is a date–fixed effect, $QP_{in}$ is an indicator variable, which is one if the firm is in price sensitivity quintile $n$; $QV_{in}$ is an indicator variable which is one if the firm is in volatility sensitivity quintile $n$; and $D_{qy}$ is an indicator variable which is one if the year $y$ is 2003 or later. The coefficient of interest is $\beta_{3n}$ where $n$ defines the quintile. These are the coefficients on the interaction of the after–tax–change dummy and quintile $n$ dummy.

The main econometric issue in estimating the previous equation is that even without tax changes, many other items may affect a firm's stock price volatility. There is a large literature on the changes to volatility over time. I take into account many of the explanations by adding the appropriate explanatory variables so the regressions are not biased by these omitted variables.[16] I control for price here as the standard deviation of price should increase

---

[16]See Campbell, Lettau, Malkiel and Xu (2001); Bennett, Sias and Starks (2003), Xu and Malkiel (2003); Fink, Fink, Grullon and Weston (2010); Brown and Kapadia (2007); Wei and Zhang (2006); Irvine and

with the price of the stock. In Table 4, I find a positive and statistically significant coefficient on price but it is not one. This difference may be because volatility is largest for prices close to zero, i.e. firms closer to bankruptcy. The coefficient on price is statistically significant at the 1% level. It is also statistically different than one at the 1% level. Therefore, there does seem to be an increase in the volatility of price as prices increases, but it does not increase one-for-one. The previous literature showed that some of the increases in volatility over the 1990s were due to an increase in the number of smaller firms. Therefore, I include the log of assets and the log of market capitalization. I find a statistically significant positive coefficient on assets in most specifications and a statistically significant negative coefficient on market capitalization. Assets measures all tangible assets of the firm. This could be financed by either equity or debt. Market capitalization only includes equity. Therefore, I find that the bigger the firm, the higher the volatility, but the higher equity financed the lower the volatility. I may be finding a measure of leverage here. I also include the log of leverage directly. However, this has the opposite sign than expected. I find a negative and statistically significant coefficient. Theory would suggest that leverage should increase volatility as less cash flows are available to equity holders. Previous literature showed that the increase in leverage over the 1990s increased overall volatility during that time period. In the same vein, I find that market–to–book values are positive and statistically significant. This may be due to newer firms that are riskier (i.e. high growth firms). I do not find an effect for profit margin when the other variables are included. Earnings per share is negatively associated with price as expected, but sales per share is positively related. If a

Pontiff (2009); Comin and Philippon (2005); Rajgopal and Venkatachalam (2011) for several examples of explanations.

firm has high sales per share but low earnings per share, the firm has low margins. This may increase volatility as the firm could be close to the break-even point often. As there may be many factors of the economy that change the overall level of volatility, I include date–fixed effects. In addition, some firms or industries may naturally have higher volatility. Therefore, I include firm–fixed effects.[17] I also include price-decile effects and allow the price-decile effects to change in 2003. These price-deciles are defined for the whole CRSP market to agree with the previous literature, not just for the S&P 1500. I also include sensitivity to volatility quintiles times the tax–change dummy. For executives who have a lot of options, the valuation of the take-home pay increases with an increase in volatility. Therefore, they have less of an incentive to decrease volatility if an executive has a large number of options. I find that the coefficient on Sensitivity to Volatility Quintile 5 times after–tax dummy is positive and statistically significant as expected. The coefficients decrease as one moves to lower quintiles, as expected, and Quintile 2 is more negative than Quintile 1. Quintile 1 only includes firms that do not have executives with options. These results agree with Hypothesis 2.

In the regressions, I use multiple samples. Column (1) always includes all firms. Column (2) includes only firms based in the United States. However, since I am looking at S&P 1500, firms this is most of the firms. Column (3) only includes financial firms. Column (4) only includes utilities. Column (5) only considers firms that are not in regulated industries (utilities and financial firms). Column (6) only considers American firms that are not in regulated industries (utilities and financial firms). Column (7) does not include quarterly observations

---

[17]In results not shown in the paper I included industry-time effects. The results are similar to the tables in the paper. I also considered a balanced panel of firms. I found similar results.

for firms that initiated a regular dividend in the quarter being examined or increased the regular dividend more than 20% in the quarter. Regulated firms may behave differently or may have limits on dividends. Therefore, I separate the two regulated industries. Also, firms who changed dividend policy during that quarter may have transition effects. Therefore, I exclude the relevant observations in Column (7).

Consistent with Hypothesis 1, I test whether a decrease in the volatility following a decrease in the tax rate on dividends is largest in magnitude for firms that previously had a large incentive scheme. Therefore, the firms with executives who are in Quintile 5 should experience a greater negative effect on volatility than the firms with executives in other quintiles. Quintile 4 should be more negative than Quintile 3, which should be more negative than Quintile 2, which should be more negative than Quintile 1. I find a negative and statistically significant coefficient on Price Quintile 5 times After Tax Change. The coefficients on each of the consecutive quintiles is smaller in magnitude. For firms in industries that are not regulated, the p-value for the difference between Quintile 5 and Quintile 4 is 0.0000. The p-value for the difference between Quintile 4 and Quintile 3 is 0.0093. The p-value for the difference between Quintile 3 and Quintile 2 is 0.0012. Therefore, Quintile 5 is statistically different than Quintile 4, Quintile 4 is statistically different than Quintile 3, and Quintile 3 is statistically different than Quintile 2. Quintile 1 and 2 are not statistically different. However, I do not find a statistically significant decrease for firms in the financial industry. Firms in the utility industry behave similarly to firms in non-regulated industries. Firms who do not change dividend policy have very similar results as all firms (-0.280 vs -0.279). Therefore, I find evidence that the volatility of all non-regulated firms and utilities decreased for firms with the highest incentives after the dividend tax change.

Table 5 illustrates the economic effects for Column (6) in the previous table. For a firm with an executive in the fifth quintile of price sensitivity who has no options (the first quintile for volatility sensitivity), the volatility would decrease 25% on average compared with a firm with very little stock based compensation. However, if the executive had options, the decrease would not be as large (for a firm with an executive in the highest volatility sensitivity quintile, the decrease would only be about 15%). Therefore, some of the cost of the tax change could be offset with higher level of options. On the other hand, if an executive has a low level of price sensitivity but a high amount of volatility sensitivity, the volatility of the firm may have increased 13%. Generally we ignore these effects. Agency costs associated with volatility might be important to consider when deciding on optimal tax policy.

Table 6 includes regressions of all four volatility measures for American firms not in regulated industries. Comparing the coefficients of interest to the benchmark, the coefficients on the return measures are smaller in magnitude than for the price measures. However, they are as statistically significant. The price control has flipped sign for the return measures, as expected. Otherwise, the coefficients are generally smaller in magnitude but have the same sign and statistical significance. Therefore, we could use other measures of volatility.

One group of firms would not be affected by the dividend tax change law but are affected by the other tax changes: firms that do not issue dividends (or do not begin to issue dividends after the tax change). Therefore, I take a triple–difference approach. I find the volatility results hold only for firms who issue dividends at some point. In Column (2) of Table 7, the coefficients on Quintile 5 times after the tax times the firm has issued dividends is negative and statistically significant for all measures of variance. The same is true for Quintile 4 and 3, but they are smaller in magnitude than Quintile 5. This is the expected result. I do not find statistically significant coefficients on Quintile 5 times after tax. Therefore, the volatility results hold for firms who issue dividends but not for firms who do not issue dividends. These are the expected results.

I have shown that the firm stock price volatility for firms with highly incentivized executives fell for highly incentivized executives relative to less incentivized executives. In addition, firms who incentive the executives with options have less of an effect.

As previously discussed, previous literature has also shown that earnings quality may impact volatility. Given the changes around 2003 (i.e. the Sarbanes Oxley Act), it may be important to control for earnings quality changes over time. These changes may differentially affect firms with larger incentives. In Column (1) of Table 7, I include an earnings quality measure as defined in Dechow and Dichev (2002). I find very similar results for the coefficients of interest.

Following previous literature, I bucketed the sensitivity to price and volatility into quintiles. However, you could also look at the linear effect. In Column (4), rather than using the sensitivity measures by quintile, I include the log of one plus sensitivity for both price and volatility. Both are significant at the one percent level and have the expected sign. The coefficient on price is larger than the coefficient on volatility. The coefficient on the sensitivity to price is -0.0556. For firms in the highest price quintile, the average log of one plus the sensitivity to price is 8.15, which would imply an average effect of -0.45, which is larger in magnitude than the quintile effect (-0.29). The equivalent calculation for volatility implies an average effect of 0.17 versus 0.13.

We may also be concerned about timing. There are several ways one can look into the timing. First, the tax rates on dividends increased slightly from 15% to 20% in 2013 only for individuals in the highest income bracket. Most executives, however, will fall into this bucket. The change is much smaller than the dividend tax change (from 35% to 15%). Although it may be too early to tell, I do not find a differential effect for 2013 in Column (3).

Additionally, I also consider a smaller time window in Column (5), only considering quarters that ended between 1999 and 2006 (four years on either side of the tax change). The coefficients of interest are smaller in magnitude (-0.258 vs -0.288 for price sensitivity quintile 5) but are as statistically significant.

Lastly I allow the timing to vary. I look at the effect on each quarter from seven quarters before January 2003 to seven quarters after. At that point I assume it has stabilized. I primarily consider the effect for the 5th Quintile, and only include the results for the Quintile 5 in Table 8, as there are too many variables for a single page. For the log standard deviation of stock price error, the effect seems to take place in Quarter 1 where Quarter 0 is defined as the quarter ending in either January, February, or March of 2003 depending on the firm fiscal year. The coefficient is negative and statistically significant from Quarter 0 on. It increases in magnitude through Quarter 4. From this, it appears that the second quarter of 2003 is the important quarter for the stock price volatility. This timing is consistent with the introduction of the change in dividend taxes in the first quarter of 2003.

# 4 Conclusion

In this paper, I empirically assess the effect of a dividend tax cut on firm stock price volatility. I find that stock volatility decreased more for firms with highly incentivized executives relative to firms with less highly incentivized executives. Specifically, I consider the idiosyncratic stock price volatility, as it is the optimal measure if overall take-home incentive pay for an executive is strongly correlated with stock price. This correlation exists when there is no strong negative correlation between the stock price and the number of shares and stock options the executive receives. In the data, I find that there is a positive correlation between overall take-home pay and stock price, which supports using this measure. In addition, the idiosyncratic volatility is the measure of volatility that an executive is most likely able to control. It is also the portion of the risk that most shareholders may be able to diversify away, but executives are unable to. I find that the idiosyncratic stock price volatility decreased for executives who have large incentive schemes relative to executives with smaller incentive schemes. These executives are the ones whose take-home pay is the most affected by the price volatility. In traditional models, where an executive does not control volatility, the volatility change should be constant for all levels of incentive pay.

I find that stock volatility decreased more for firms with highly incentivized executives relative to firms with less highly incentivized executives. This finding suggests that we may want to consider the effects on firm stock price volatility in addition to the overall effects on the stock price when we discuss changes to tax policy. Often when we talk about changing a tax, we only talk about the effect on the mean. We do not often talk about the effect on the variance. However, when discussing corporate taxes, the variance can be important, especially in a world with agency costs due to the hiring of a manager. If the manager is risk-averse, he will be negatively affected by the variance. If he has a high level of incentives, he will want to take actions to reduce the variance or decrease his take-home pay's dependence on the stock price. By decreasing his dependence on take-home incentive pay, he also has less of an incentive to increase firm value, thereby increasing agency costs. If decreasing variance can only be done in a way that destructs firm value destructing, then this will also lead to larger agency costs. My findings are in line with an agency cost model. I find the tax cut decreased variance unevenly across firms. Therefore, corporate taxes may affect the volatility of some firms more than others. Increasing the portion of the compensation package that is comprised of options would offset some of these costs.

Future work in optimal tax policy should consider the agency costs associated with changes to the variance of a stock price. Changes to personal taxes as well as corporate taxes could affect the agency costs. Therefore, the effects on the variance of a stock should be included in tax-code optimization.

# References

**Aggarwal, Rajesh and Andrew A. Samwick**, "The Other Side of the Trade-Off: The Impact of Risk on Executive Compensation," *Journal of Political Economy*, February 1999, *107* (1), 65–105.

**Amromin, Gene, Paul Harrison, and Steven Sharpe**, "How Did the 2003 Dividend Tax Cut Affect Stock Prices?," *Financial Management*, Winter 2008, *37* (4), 625–646.

**Auerbach, Alan J.**, "Taxation and Corporate Financial Policy," in Alan J. Auerbach and Martin Feldstein, eds., *Handbook of Public Economics*, Vol. 3, Elsevier Science B.V., 2002, chapter 19, pp. 1251–1292.

____ **and Kevin A. Hassett**, "The 2003 Dividend Tax Cuts and the Value of the Firm: An Event Study," *NBER Working Paper 11449*, June 2005.

**Auten, Gerald, Robert Carroll, and Geoffrey Gee**, "The 2001 and 2003 Tax Rate Reductions: An Overview and Estimate of the Taxable Income Response," *National Tax Journal*, September 2008, *61* (3), 345–364.

**Bennett, James A., Richard W. Sias, and Laura T. Starks**, "Greener Pastures and the Impact of Dynamic Institutional Preferences," *The Review of Financial Studies*, Winter 2003, *16* (4), 1203–1238.

**Bernheim, B. Douglas and Adam Wantz**, "A Tax-Based Test of the Dividend Signaling Hypothesis," *The American Economic Review*, June 1995, *85* (3), 532–551.

____ **and Lee S. Redding**, "Optimal Money Burning: Theory and Application to Corporate Dividends," *Journal of Economics and Management Strategy*, Winter 2001, *10* (4), 463–507.

**Blouin, Jennifer L., Jana Smith Raedy, and Douglas A. Shackelford**, "Did Firms Substitute Dividends for Share Repurchases After the 2003 Reductions in Shareholder Tax Rates?," *NBER Working Paper 13601*, November 2007.

**Brown, Gregory and Nishad Kapadia**, "Firm-Specific Risk and Equity Market Development," *Journal of Financial Economics*, May 2007, *84* (2), 358–388.

**Brown, Jeffrey R., Nellie Liang, and Scott Weisbenner**, "Executive Financial Incentives and Payout Policy: Firm Responses to the 2003 Dividend Tax Cut," *The Journal of Finance*, August 2007, *62* (4), 1935–1965.

**Campbell, John Y., Martin Lettau, Burton G. Malkiel, and Yexiao Xu**, "Have Individual Stocks Become More Volatile? An Empirical Exploration of Idiosyncratic Risk," *The Journal of Finance*, February 2001, *56* (1), 1–43.

**Chava, Sudheer and Amiyatosh Purnanandam**, "CEOs versus CFOs: Incentives and Corporate Policies," *Journal of Financial Economics*, August 2010, *97* (2), 263–278.

**Chetty, Raj and Emmanuel Saez**, "Dividend Taxes and Corporate Behavior: Evidence from the 2003 Tax Cut," *Quarterly Journal of Economics*, August 2005, *120* (3), 791–833.

＿ **and** ＿ , "Dividend and Corporate Taxation in an Agency Model of the Firm," *American Economic Journal: Economic Policy*, August 2010, *2* (3), 1–31.

**Christie, William G. and Vikram Nanda**, "Free Cash Flow, Shareholder Value, and the Undistributed Profits Tax of 1936 and 1937," *The Journal of Finance*, December 1994, *49* (5), 1727–1754.

**Coles, Jeffrey L., Naveen D. Daniel, and Lalitha Naveen**, "Managerial Incentives and Risk-Taking," *Journal of Financial Economics*, February 2006, *79* (2), 431–468.

**Comin, Diego A. and Thomas Philippon**, "The Rise in Firm-Level Volatility: Causes and Consequences," *NBER Macroeconomics Annual*, 2005.

**Core, John E. and Wayne R. Guay**, "The Use of Equity Grants to Manage Optimal Equity Incentive Levels," *Journal of Accounting and Economics*, December 1999, *28* (2), 151–184.

＿ **and** ＿ , "Estimating the Value of Employee Stock Option Portfolios and Their Sensitivities to Price and Volatility," *Journal of Accounting Research*, June 2002, *40* (3), 613–630.

＿ **and** ＿ , "The Other Side of the Trade-Off: The Impact of Risk on Executive Compensation - A Revised Comment," 2002. Working Paper.

**Dechow, Patricia M. and Ilia D. Dichev**, "The Quality of Accruals and Earnings: The Role of Accrual Estimation Errors," *The Accounting Review*, 2002, *77* (s-1), 35–59.

**Fama, Eugene F. and Kenneth R. French**, "Common Risk Factors in the Returns on Stocks and Bonds," *Journal of Financial Economics*, February 1993, *33* (1), 3–56.

**Fenn, George W. and Nellie Liang**, "Corporate Payout Policy and Managerial Stock Incentives," *Journal of Financial Economics*, April 2001, *60* (1), 45–72.

**Fink, Jason, Kristin E. Fink, Gustavo Grullon, and James P. Weston**, "What Drove the Increase in Idiosyncratic Volatility during the Internet Boom?," *Journal of Financial and Quantitative Analysis*, October 2010, *45* (5), 1253–1278.

**Frydman, Carola and Dirk Jenter**, "CEO Compensation," *Annual Review of Financial Economics*, December 2010, *2* (1), 75–102.

**Gordon, Roger and Martin Dietz**, "Dividend and Taxes," *NBER Working Paper 12292*, June 2006.

**Graham, John R.**, "Debt and the Marginal Tax Rate," *Journal of Financial Economics*, May 1996, *41* (1), 41–74.

_____ , "Taxes and Corporate Finance: A Review," *The Review of Financial Studies*, Winter 2003, *16* (4), 1075–1129.

**Hirshleifer, David and Yoon Suh**, "Risk, Managerial Effort, and Project Choice," *Journal of Financial Intermediations*, September 1992, *2* (3), 308–345.

**Irvine, Paul J. and Jeffrey Pontiff**, "Idiosyncratic Return Volatility, Cash Flows, and Product Market Competition," *The Review of Financial Studies*, March 2009, *22* (3), 1149–1177.

**Jensen, Michael C. and William H. Meckling**, "Theory of the Firm: Managerial Behavior, Agency Costs, and Ownership Structure," *Journal of Financial Economics*, October 1976, *3* (4), 305–360.

**Jin, Li**, "CEO Compensation, Diversification, and Incentives," *Journal of Financial Economics*, October 2002, *66* (1), 29–63.

**Knopf, John D., Jouahn Nam, and John H. Thorton Jr.**, "The Volatility and Price Sensitivities of Managerial Stock Option Portfolios and Corporate Hedging," *The Journal of Finance*, April 2002, *57* (2), 801–813.

**La Porta, Rafael, Florencio Lopez de Silanes, Andrei Schleifer, and Robert W. Vishny**, "Agency Problems and Dividend Policies around the World," *The Journal of Finance*, February 2000, *55* (1), 1–33.

**Lambert, Richard A.**, "Executive Effort and Selection of Risky Projects," *RAND Journal of Economics*, Spring 1986, *17* (1), 77–88.

**MacKie-Mason, Jeffrey K.**, "Do Taxes Affect Corporate Financing Decisions?," *The Journal of Finance*, December 1990, *45* (5), 1471–1493.

**Malmendier, Ulrike and Geoffrey Tate**, "Superstar CEOs," *Quarterly Journal of Economics*, November 2009, *124* (4), 1593–1638.

**Modigliani, Franco and Merton H. Miller**, "The Cost of Capital, Corporation Finance and the Theory of Investment," *The American Economic Review*, June 1958, *48* (3), 261–297.

**Murphy, Kevin J.**, "Executive Compensation," in Orley C. Ashenfelter and David Card, eds., *Handbook of Labor Economics*, Vol. 3B, Elsevier Science B.V., 1999, chapter 38, pp. 2485–2566.

**Nam, Jouahn, Jun Wang, and Ge Zhang**, "The Impact of Dividend Tax Cut and Managerial Stock Holdings on Firm's Dividend Policy," *EFMA 2004 Basel Meetings Paper*, January 2004.

**Rajgopal, Shiva and Mohan Venkatachalam**, "Financial Reporting Quality and Idiosyncratic Return Volatility," *Journal of Accounting and Economics*, February 2011, *51* (1-2), 1–20.

**Stein, Jeremy C.**, "Agency, Information, and Corporate Investment," *NBER Working Paper 8342*, June 2001.

**Tirole, Jean**, *The Theory of Corporate Finance*, Princeton, New Jersey: Princeton University Press, 2006.

**Wei, Steven X. and Chu Zhang**, "Why did Individual Stocks Become More Volatile," *The Journal of Business*, January 2006, *79* (1), 259–292.

**Xu, Yexiao and Burton G. Malkiel**, "Investigating the Behavior of Idiosyncratic Volatility," *The Journal of Business*, October 2003, *76* (4), 613–645.

# 5 Figures and Tables

## Table 1: Firm Summary Statistics

|                    | Count  | Mean      | Std. Dev.  | Min     | Max           |
|--------------------|--------|-----------|------------|---------|---------------|
| Price              | 88,457 | 82.4      | 2,035      | 0.05    | 141,600       |
| Total Assets       | 88,457 | 15,762    | 87,539     | 5.123   | 3,256,267     |
| Market Cap         | 88,457 | 8,280     | 25,881     | 2.69325 | 626,550       |
| Profit Margin      | 88,457 | 0.07      | 0.15       | -1.00   | 10.05         |
| Earnings per Share | 88,457 | 1.08      | 31.00      | -1.00   | 3330          |
| Sales per Share    | 88,457 | 36.0      | 772.2      | -0.8    | 76222.9       |
| Return on Assets   | 88,457 | 0.03      | 0.06       | -0.98   | 2.17          |
| Market to Book     | 88,457 | 1.86      | 1.47       | 0.30    | 74.46         |
| Leverage Ratio     | 88,457 | 0.19      | 0.17       | 0.00    | 2.71          |
| Earnings Quality   | 59,639 | 1,948,552 | 19,200,000 | 0       | 1,280,000,000 |

Source: Wharton Research Database Services (WRDS): Center for Research in Security Prices (CRSP) and Compusat

## Figure 1: Volatility Measures

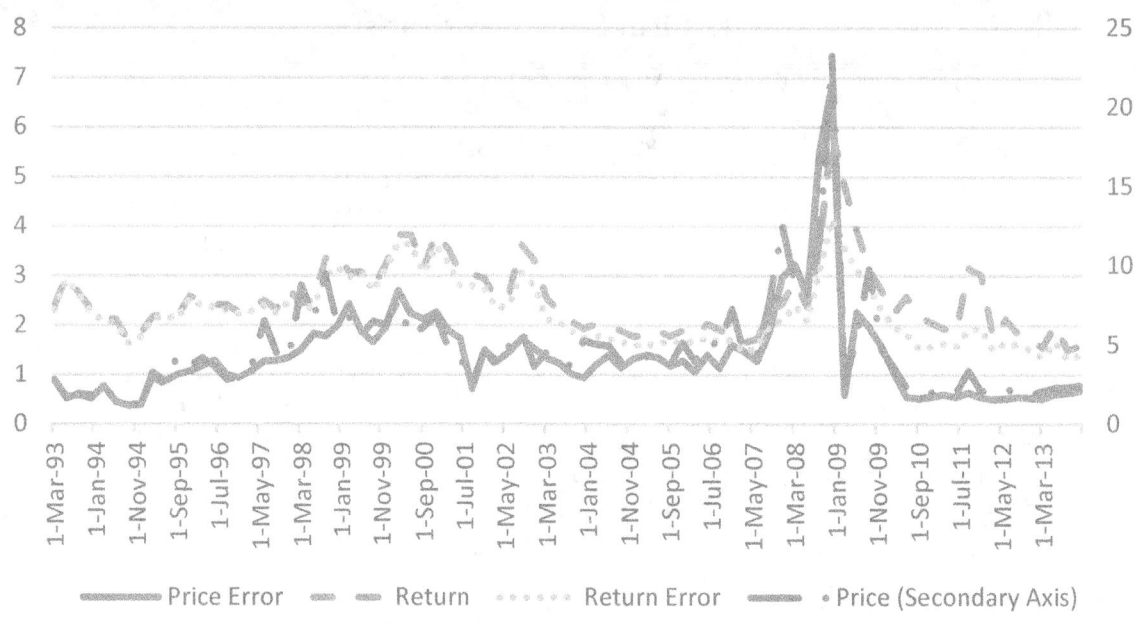

Price Error — Return · · · · Return Error — Price (Secondary Axis)

Source: Wharton Research Database Services (WRDS): Center for Research in Security Prices (CRSP)

## Table 2: Sensitivity Measures Summary Statistics

Sensitivity to Price by Sensitivity to Price Qntiles

| Quant | Count | Mean | Std Dev | Min | Max |
|-------|-------|--------|---------|--------|----------|
| 1 | 293 | 14.94 | 11.48 | 0.00 | 39.64 |
| 2 | 293 | 85.13 | 28.13 | 40.58 | 137.52 |
| 3 | 293 | 244.28 | 67.17 | 137.74 | 371.03 |
| 4 | 293 | 688.39 | 220.42 | 377.17 | 1,161.54 |
| 5 | 293 | 9,783 | 42,167 | 1,165 | 585,400 |

Sensitivity to Volatility by Sensitivity to Vol Qntiles

| Quant | Count | Mean | Std Dev | Min | Max |
|-------|-------|--------|---------|----------|-------|
| 1 | 507 | 0.00 | 0.00 | 0.00 | 0.00 |
| 2 | 79 | 0.29 | 0.31 | 1.05E-30 | 0.99 |
| 3 | 293 | 6.79 | 4.10 | 1.04 | 14.52 |
| 4 | 293 | 31.26 | 12.04 | 14.61 | 54.50 |
| 5 | 293 | 184.50 | 297.22 | 54.54 | 4,536 |

Source: Wharton Research Database Services (WRDS): Compusat ExecuComp

**Table 3: Sensitivity Quantile Summary Statistics**

| Price | Volatility | | | | | Total |
|---|---|---|---|---|---|---|
| | 1 | 2 | 3 | 4 | 5 | |
| 1 | 219 | 15 | 55 | 4 | 0 | 293 |
| 2 | 108 | 18 | 63 | 87 | 17 | 293 |
| 3 | 64 | 15 | 66 | 81 | 67 | 293 |
| 4 | 59 | 16 | 50 | 67 | 101 | 293 |
| 5 | 57 | 15 | 59 | 54 | 108 | 293 |

Source: Wharton Research Database Services (WRDS): Compusat ExecuComp

## Table 4: Log Standard Deviation of Stock Price Error

|  | (1) | (2) | (3) | (4) | (5) | (6) | (7) |
|---|---|---|---|---|---|---|---|
| Price Qnt 5 * After Tax | -0.280*** | -0.279*** | -0.185** | -0.265*** | -0.295*** | -0.293*** | -0.279*** |
|  | (0.0300) | (0.0302) | (0.0782) | (0.0960) | (0.0332) | (0.0336) | (0.0305) |
| Price Qnt 4 * After Tax | -0.122*** | -0.124*** | -0.0180 | -0.0930 | -0.139*** | -0.142*** | -0.119*** |
|  | (0.0287) | (0.0290) | (0.0746) | (0.0888) | (0.0319) | (0.0323) | (0.0292) |
| Price Qnt 3 * After Tax | -0.0831*** | -0.0804*** | -0.0280 | -0.133* | -0.0805*** | -0.0765** | -0.0851*** |
|  | (0.0266) | (0.0267) | (0.0704) | (0.0732) | (0.0299) | (0.0301) | (0.0270) |
| Price Qnt 2 * After Tax | 0.00314 | 0.00416 | -0.0771 | 0.00668 | 0.00475 | 0.00610 | 0.00111 |
|  | (0.0263) | (0.0264) | (0.0790) | (0.0682) | (0.0293) | (0.0295) | (0.0268) |
| Log Price | 0.715*** | 0.717*** | 0.630*** | 0.689*** | 0.723*** | 0.725*** | 0.715*** |
|  | (0.0258) | (0.0263) | (0.0402) | (0.0601) | (0.0302) | (0.0308) | (0.0280) |
| Log Assets | 0.188*** | 0.188*** | 0.100*** | 0.362*** | 0.200*** | 0.200*** | 0.188*** |
|  | (0.0147) | (0.0149) | (0.0285) | (0.0612) | (0.0179) | (0.0180) | (0.0151) |
| Log Market Cap | -0.153*** | -0.153*** | -0.0293 | -0.291*** | -0.172*** | -0.172*** | -0.153*** |
|  | (0.0165) | (0.0168) | (0.0363) | (0.0704) | (0.0199) | (0.0201) | (0.0170) |
| Log Profit Margin | -0.0159 | -0.0175 | -0.0267 | -0.360** | 0.000201 | -0.000668 | -0.0136 |
|  | (0.0143) | (0.0146) | (0.0540) | (0.144) | (0.0142) | (0.0145) | (0.0146) |
| Log EPS | -0.0381*** | -0.0384*** | -0.0743*** | -0.00784 | -0.0280*** | -0.0282*** | -0.0409*** |
|  | (0.00557) | (0.00566) | (0.0188) | (0.0143) | (0.00604) | (0.00612) | (0.00590) |
| Log Sales PS | 0.0352*** | 0.0349*** | 0.0764*** | -0.0338* | 0.0348*** | 0.0346*** | 0.0342*** |
|  | (0.00471) | (0.00476) | (0.0184) | (0.0189) | (0.00491) | (0.00496) | (0.00490) |
| Log ROA | 0.0117 | 0.0133 | -0.299 | 2.134*** | -0.0298 | -0.0292 | 0.0230 |
|  | (0.0376) | (0.0379) | (0.208) | (0.717) | (0.0375) | (0.0378) | (0.0387) |
| Log Market to Book | 0.694*** | 0.692*** | 0.924*** | 1.887*** | 0.682*** | 0.681*** | 0.690*** |
|  | (0.0255) | (0.0259) | (0.116) | (0.255) | (0.0294) | (0.0296) | (0.0264) |
| Log Leverage | -0.234*** | -0.236*** | -0.189* | -0.819*** | -0.246*** | -0.248*** | -0.230*** |
|  | (0.0409) | (0.0412) | (0.107) | (0.196) | (0.0439) | (0.0443) | (0.0419) |
| Vol Qnt 2 * After Tax | -0.0949*** | -0.0928** | -0.242*** |  | -0.0937** | -0.0914** | -0.0940** |
|  | (0.0362) | (0.0362) | (0.0645) |  | (0.0414) | (0.0415) | (0.0366) |
| Vol Qnt 3 * After Tax | 0.0642*** | 0.0646*** | -0.131** | 0.00725 | 0.0793*** | 0.0791*** | 0.0657*** |
|  | (0.0243) | (0.0244) | (0.0615) | (0.0567) | (0.0280) | (0.0282) | (0.0247) |
| Vol Qnt 4 * After Tax | 0.0979*** | 0.102*** | -0.146** | 0.0290 | 0.129*** | 0.134*** | 0.104*** |
|  | (0.0222) | (0.0225) | (0.0582) | (0.0569) | (0.0247) | (0.0250) | (0.0226) |
| Vol Qnt 5 * After Tax | 0.112*** | 0.112*** | -0.131** | 0.0412 | 0.126*** | 0.125*** | 0.112*** |
|  | (0.0241) | (0.0245) | (0.0658) | (0.0591) | (0.0276) | (0.0282) | (0.0244) |
| Constant | -4.003*** | -4.009*** | -4.341*** | -4.836*** | -3.874*** | -3.879*** | -4.008*** |
|  | (0.0749) | (0.0763) | (0.284) | (0.342) | (0.0784) | (0.0796) | (0.0759) |
| Observations | 88,457 | 86,927 | 11,852 | 6,208 | 70,397 | 69,073 | 81,666 |
| R-squared | 0.597 | 0.596 | 0.548 | 0.557 | 0.620 | 0.619 | 0.597 |
| Number of Firms | 1,512 | 1,487 | 202 | 91 | 1,222 | 1,201 | 1,507 |

*Notes:* Clustered standard errors in parentheses. Column (1) includes all firms. Column (2) includes only firms based in the United States. Column (3) only includes financial firms. Column (4) only includes utilities. Column (5) only considers firms that are not in regulated industries (utilities and financial firms). Column (6) only considers American firms that are not in regulated industries (utilities and financial firms). Column (7) does not include quarterly observations for firms that initiated a regular dividend in the quarter being examined or increased the regular dividend more that 20% in the quarter.
*** p<0.01, ** p<0.05, * p<0.1

## Table 5: Economic Effects

| Price | Volatility | | | | |
|---|---|---|---|---|---|
| | 1 | 2 | 3 | 4 | 5 |
| 1 | 1.00 | 0.91 | 1.08 | 1.14 | 1.13 |
| | (1.000) | (0.028) | (0.005) | (0.000) | (0.000) |
| 2 | 1.01 | 0.92 | 1.09 | 1.15 | 1.14 |
| | (0.836) | (0.067) | (0.020) | (0.000) | (0.000) |
| 3 | 0.93 | 0.85 | 1.00 | 1.06 | 1.05 |
| | (0.011) | (0.000) | (0.940) | (0.058) | (0.145) |
| 4 | 0.87 | 0.79 | 0.94 | 0.99 | 0.98 |
| | (0.000) | (0.000) | (0.084) | (0.799) | (0.609) |
| 5 | 0.75 | 0.68 | 0.81 | 0.85 | 0.85 |
| | (0.000) | (0.000) | (0.000) | (0.000) | (0.000) |

P-values in parentheses.

## Table 6: All Standard Deviation Measures

| | Log Std. Dev. Price Error | Log Std. Dev. Price | Log Std. Dev. Return | Log Std. Dev. Return Error |
|---|---|---|---|---|
| Price Quant 5 * After Tax | -0.293*** | -0.289*** | -0.251*** | -0.232*** |
| | (0.0336) | (0.0331) | (0.0310) | (0.0305) |
| Price Quant 4 * After Tax | -0.142*** | -0.148*** | -0.116*** | -0.111*** |
| | (0.0323) | (0.0316) | (0.0295) | (0.0293) |
| Price Quant 3 * After Tax | -0.0765** | -0.0704** | -0.0509* | -0.0593** |
| | (0.0301) | (0.0301) | (0.0278) | (0.0274) |
| Price Quant 2 * After Tax | 0.00610 | 0.00810 | 0.0267 | 0.0161 |
| | (0.0295) | (0.0295) | (0.0276) | (0.0273) |
| Log Price | 0.725*** | 0.791*** | -0.131*** | -0.161*** |
| | (0.0308) | (0.0245) | (0.0212) | (0.0252) |
| Log Assets | 0.200*** | 0.300*** | 0.150*** | 0.157*** |
| | (0.0180) | (0.0183) | (0.0163) | (0.0171) |
| Log Market Cap | -0.172*** | -0.263*** | -0.166*** | -0.189*** |
| | (0.0201) | (0.0194) | (0.0177) | (0.0194) |
| Log Profit Margin | -0.000668 | -0.00497 | -0.0118 | -0.00777 |
| | (0.0145) | (0.0179) | (0.0152) | (0.0156) |
| Log EPS | -0.0282*** | -0.0322*** | -0.0294*** | -0.0247*** |
| | (0.00612) | (0.00734) | (0.00550) | (0.00565) |
| Log Sales PS | 0.0346*** | 0.0145*** | 0.0115** | 0.0229*** |
| | (0.00496) | (0.00557) | (0.00454) | (0.00450) |
| Log ROA | -0.0292 | -0.151*** | -0.122*** | -0.124*** |
| | (0.0378) | (0.0469) | (0.0352) | (0.0349) |
| Log Market to Book | 0.681*** | 0.793*** | 0.627*** | 0.649*** |
| | (0.0296) | (0.0316) | (0.0262) | (0.0273) |
| Log Leverage | -0.248*** | -0.218*** | -0.169*** | -0.171*** |
| | (0.0443) | (0.0454) | (0.0418) | (0.0421) |
| Vol Qnt 2 * After Tax | -0.0914** | -0.0909** | -0.0200 | -0.0446 |
| | (0.0415) | (0.0438) | (0.0417) | (0.0374) |
| Vol Qnt 3 * After Tax | 0.0791*** | 0.0985*** | 0.107*** | 0.0912*** |
| | (0.0282) | (0.0277) | (0.0254) | (0.0256) |
| Vol Qnt 4 * After Tax | 0.134*** | 0.162*** | 0.153*** | 0.128*** |
| | (0.0250) | (0.0245) | (0.0235) | (0.0229) |
| Vol Qnt 5 * After Tax | 0.125*** | 0.172*** | 0.142*** | 0.117*** |
| | (0.0282) | (0.0258) | (0.0256) | (0.0255) |
| Constant | -3.879*** | -3.362*** | -3.797*** | -3.784*** |
| | (0.0796) | (0.0873) | (0.0770) | (0.0756) |
| | | | | |
| Observations | 69,073 | 69,073 | 69,073 | 69,073 |
| R-squared | 0.619 | 0.532 | 0.448 | 0.443 |
| Number of Firms | 1,201 | 1,201 | 1,201 | 1,201 |

*Notes:* Clustered standard errors in parentheses. All columns only considers American firms that are not in regulated industries (utilities and financial firms)
*** p<0.01, ** p<0.05, * p<0.1

## Table 7: Robustness Checks: Log Standard Deviation of Stock Price Error

|  | (1) | (2) | (3) | (4) | (5) |
|---|---|---|---|---|---|
| Price Qnt 5 * After Tax | -0.318*** | -0.0730 | -0.294*** |  | -0.262*** |
|  | (0.0354) | (0.0518) | (0.0333) |  | (0.0282) |
| Price Qnt 4 * After Tax | -0.170*** | 0.00589 | -0.142*** |  | -0.144*** |
|  | (0.0335) | (0.0546) | (0.0320) |  | (0.0278) |
| Price Qnt 3 * After Tax | -0.0988*** | 0.0130 | -0.0761** |  | -0.0995*** |
|  | (0.0321) | (0.0439) | (0.0298) |  | (0.0251) |
| Price Qnt 2 * After Tax | -0.00705 | -0.0300 | 0.00830 |  | -0.0125 |
|  | (0.0313) | (0.0418) | (0.0294) |  | (0.0253) |
| Price Qnt 5 * After Tax * Div Pay |  | -0.285*** |  |  |  |
|  |  | (0.0668) |  |  |  |
| Price Qnt 4 * After Tax * Div Pay |  | -0.198*** |  |  |  |
|  |  | (0.0673) |  |  |  |
| Price Qnt 3 * After Tax * Div Pay |  | -0.115** |  |  |  |
|  |  | (0.0584) |  |  |  |
| Price Qnt 2 * After Tax * Div Pay |  | 0.0166 |  |  |  |
|  |  | (0.0571) |  |  |  |
| Price Qnt 5 * 2013 Year |  |  | -0.0154 |  |  |
|  |  |  | (0.0402) |  |  |
| Price Qnt 4 * 2013 Year |  |  | 0.00477 |  |  |
|  |  |  | (0.0407) |  |  |
| Price Qnt 3 * 2013 Year |  |  | -0.00814 |  |  |
|  |  |  | (0.0413) |  |  |
| Price Qnt 2 * 2013 Year |  |  | -0.0400 |  |  |
|  |  |  | (0.0413) |  |  |
| Log Price Sens. * After Tax |  |  |  | -0.0556*** |  |
|  |  |  |  | (0.00549) |  |
| Log Vol Sens. * After Tax |  |  |  | 0.0347*** |  |
|  |  |  |  | (0.00525) |  |
| Earnings Quality | 0 |  |  |  |  |
|  | (1.64e-10) |  |  |  |  |
| Constant | -4.066*** | -3.877*** | -3.880*** | -3.862*** | -4.375*** |
|  | (0.175) | (0.0773) | (0.0797) | (0.0801) | (0.173) |
|  |  |  |  |  |  |
| Observations | 53,415 | 64,732 | 69,073 | 69,073 | 32,205 |
| R-squared | 0.612 | 0.619 | 0.619 | 0.618 | 0.615 |
| Number of Firms | 1,144 | 1,196 | 1,201 | 1,201 | 1,171 |

*Notes:* Clustered standard errors in parentheses. All columns include American firms in non-regulated industries. Column (1) includes an earnings quality measure. Column (2) is a triple difference based on firms that pay a dividend. Column (3) allows for a differential effect in 2013, when tax rates changed slightly. Column (4) allows for a linear in logs effect rather than the quintile effect. Column (5) only contains quarters ending in 1999 to 2006.
*** $p<0.01$, ** $p<0.05$, * $p<0.1$

## Table 8: Timing Robustness Check

|  | (1) |
|---|---|
| Price Quint 5 * Quarter -7 | 0.0542 |
|  | (0.0431) |
| Price Quint 5 * Quarter -6 | -0.0282 |
|  | (0.0470) |
| Price Quint 5 * Quarter -5 | -0.0245 |
|  | (0.0437) |
| Price Quint 5 * Quarter -4 | -0.136*** |
|  | (0.0383) |
| Price Quint 5 * Quarter -3 | -0.120*** |
|  | (0.0411) |
| Price Quint 5 * Quarter -2 | -0.0264 |
|  | (0.0491) |
| Price Quint 5 * Quarter -1 | -0.0268 |
|  | (0.0419) |
| Price Quint 5 * Quarter 0 | -0.0674* |
|  | (0.0369) |
| Price Quint 5 * Quarter 1 | -0.122*** |
|  | (0.0438) |
| Price Quint 5 * Quarter 2 | -0.170*** |
|  | (0.0423) |
| Price Quint 5 * Quarter 3 | -0.191*** |
|  | (0.0499) |
| Price Quint 5 * Quarter 4 | -0.248*** |
|  | (0.0505) |
| Price Quint 5 * Quarter 5 | -0.250*** |
|  | (0.0471) |
| Price Quint 5 * Quarter 6 | -0.281*** |
|  | (0.0521) |
| Price Quint 5 * Quarter 7 | -0.186*** |
|  | (0.0513) |
| Price Quint 5 * 2+ Years | -0.326*** |
|  | (0.0406) |
| Constant | -3.850*** |
|  | (0.0861) |
|  |  |
| Observations | 69,073 |
| Number of Firms | 1,201 |
| R-squared | 0.622 |

*Notes:* Clustered standard errors in parentheses.
*** p<0.01, ** p<0.05, * p<0.1

# A  Appendix

## A.1  Volatility Definitions

The first measure of volatility is the standard deviation of the price. It is defined as:

$$sd(p)_{iqy} = \sqrt{\sum_{t=1}^{T}(p_{itqy} - \frac{\sum_{t=1}^{T}p_{itqy}}{T})^2} \tag{2}$$

where $p_{itqy}$ is the price of stock $i$ at day $t$ in fiscal quarter $q$ in fiscal year $y$. This measure includes both the systematic and idiosyncratic volatility.

The second measure of volatility is the standard deviation of the return. It is defined as:

$$sd(R)_{iqy} = \sqrt{\sum_{t=1}^{T}(R_{itqy} - \frac{\sum_{t=1}^{T}R_{itqy}}{T})^2} \tag{3}$$

where $R_{itqy}$ is the daily stock price return for stock $i$ for day $t$ in fiscal quarter $q$ in fiscal year $y$. This measure includes both the systematic and idiosyncratic volatility. It measures the return rather than the price.

The third and fourth measure of volatility both consider the excess standard deviation of the firm. In order to determine the excess standard deviation, one first needs to determine either the excess price changes or the excess return. In order to determine both, I estimate the expected return for the stock using the Fama-French Three-Factor Model.[18] I estimate the following equation using ordinary least squares for each fiscal year.

$$R_{itqy} - Rf_{tqy} = \alpha_{iy} + \beta_{1iy}(R_{mtqy} - Rf_{tqy}) + \beta_{2iy}SMB_{tqy} + \beta_{3iy}HML_{tqy} + \epsilon_{itqy} \tag{4}$$

where $R_{itqy}$ is the daily stock price return for stock $i$ for day $t$ in fiscal quarter $q$ in fiscal year $y$, $Rf_{tqy}$ is the risk free rate for day $t$ in fiscal quarter $q$ in fiscal year $y$, $R_{mtqy}$ is the market return for day $t$ is fiscal quarter $q$ in fiscal year $y$, $SMB_{tqy}$ is the Fama-French Small Minus Big factor for day $t$ is fiscal quarter $q$ in fiscal year $y$, and $HML_{tqy}$ is the Fama-French High Minus Low factor for day $t$ is fiscal quarter $q$ in fiscal year $y$. I then use these estimated betas to find the predicted return:

$$\hat{R_{itqy}} = Rf_{tqy} + \hat{\alpha_{iy}} + \hat{\beta_{1iy}}(R_{mtqy} + Rf_{tqy}) - \hat{\beta_{2iy}}SMB_{tqy} + \hat{\beta_{3iy}}HML_{tqy} \tag{5}$$

and the predicted price:

$$\hat{p_{itqy}} = p_{i(t-1)qy}(1 + Rf_{tqy} + \hat{\alpha_{iy}} - \hat{\beta_{1iy}}(R_{mtqy} - Rf_{tqy}) - \hat{\beta_{2iy}}SMB_{tqy} - \hat{\beta_{3iy}}HML_{tqy}) \tag{6}$$

The excess return is therefore

$$\hat{\epsilon_{itqy}} = R_{itqy} - Rf_{tqy} - \hat{\alpha_{iy}} - \hat{\beta_{1iy}}(R_{mtqy} - Rf_{tqy}) - \hat{\beta_{2iy}}SMB_{tqy} - \hat{\beta_{3iy}}HML_{tqy} \tag{7}$$

---

[18]See Fama and French (1993) for a full description of the model.

and the excess price is

$$\Delta p_{itqy} = p_{itqy} - \hat{p_{itqy}} \tag{8}$$

Now that we have measures of excess return and excess price, one can find the standard deviation of both. The third measure of volatility is the standard deviation of the return error from the Fama-French regressions:

$$sd(\hat{\epsilon})_{iqy} = \sqrt{\sum_{t=1}^{T}(\hat{\epsilon_{itqy}} - \frac{\sum_{t=1}^{T}\hat{\epsilon_{itqy}}}{T})^2} \tag{9}$$

This measure includes only the idiosyncratic volatility. It also is measured by the return rather than the price.

Finally the last measure of volatility is the standard deviation of the difference between price and expected price based on the Fama-French model:

$$sd(\Delta p)_{iqy} = \sqrt{\sum_{t=1}^{T}(\Delta p_{itqy} - \frac{\sum_{t=1}^{T}\Delta p_{itqy}}{T})^2} \tag{10}$$

This measure also only includes idiosyncratic volatility. It is measured by the price rather than the return. I focus on this measure as there is a positive correlation between executive incentive levels and stock price.